Progressive Piano Method for Young Beginners Book 3

by Andrew Scott and Gary Turner
Illustrated by James Stewart

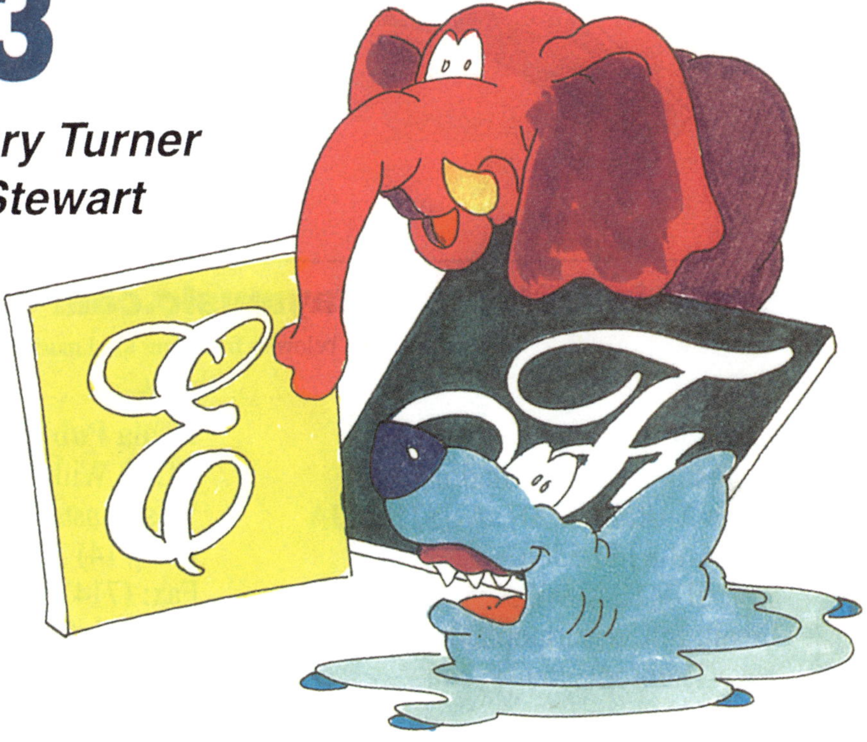

Let's Practice Together

We have recorded all the songs in this book onto a CD. When your teacher's not there, instead of practicing by yourself, you can play along with us. Playing will be much more fun, and you will learn faster. On the recording each song is played on the left hand channel. An accompaniment (to play along with) is on the right hand channel. Each song is played four times.
- The first two times contain the song with the accompaniment.
- The third and fourth times contain just the accompaniment.

The exercises in this book have been recorded onto a CD

For further details on how to purchase this recording, or other Books, CD's, DVD's and Videos in this series, contact

Email: info@learntoplaymusic.com or visit our web page on: www.learntoplaymusic.com

Contents

Introduction	Page 4
Lesson 1	**Page 5**
The C Chord	5
Careful Canary	5
The G Seventh Chord	6
Vanilla Gorilla	6
Changing Chords	7
Two Chord Tango	7
Lesson 2	**Page 8**
Songs with Chords	8
All Together Now	8
Two Chord Waltz	8
Ode To Joy	9
Buffalo Gals	10
Lesson 3	**Page 12**
The F Chord	12
Gone Fishing	12
Something Fishy	12
On Top of Old Smoky	13
Camptown Races	14
Lesson 4	**Page 16**
The G Chord	16
What's Gnu?	16
The Note F♯ (on the Bass Staff)	17
Sharp Turn	17
The D7 Chord	18
Donkey Dance	18
Seven Drowsy Donkeys	18
How Dry I Am	19
Lesson 5	**Page 20**
The Note D	20
Lightly Row	20
The G Position	22
My House	23
Lesson 6	**Page 24**
The Note F♯ (on the Treble Staff)	24
Two Sharp	24
Playing Parts of Chords	25
The William Tell Overture	25
Ten Little Indians	26
Lesson 7	**Page 27**
C Chord - 2nd Inversion	27
C What I Mean	27
Spare Change	28
Beautiful Brown Eyes	28
Lesson 8	**Page 30**
D7 Chord (Another Fingering)	30
Aloha Oe	30
Changing Between C and D7	32
Ding Dong Merrily on High	32
Lesson 9	**Page 33**
Broken Chords	33
C Saw	33
Broken Up	33
Roses from the South	34
G7 Chord (Another Fingering)	36
Breaking Up is Hard to Do	36
The Galway Piper	36
Lesson 10	**Page 38**
The Note B♭	38
Bee Flat	38
Blow the Man Down	39
Lesson 11	**Page 40**
The Note B♭ (below Middle C)	40
Blues for a Bee	40
Go Round and Round the Village	41
Dry Bones	42
Notes, Rests and Chords	44

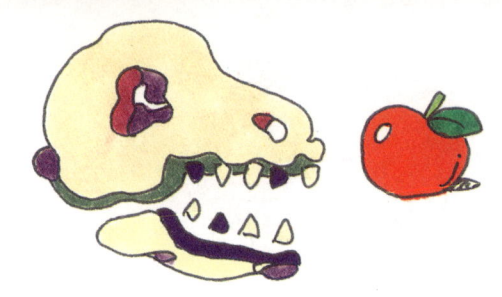

Introduction

Progressive Piano Method for Young Beginners, comprising three Method Books and three Supplementary Songbooks has been designed to introduce the younger student to the basics of piano playing and reading music.

To maximise the student's enjoyment and interest, the Progressive Young Beginner series incorporates an extensive repertoire of well-known children's songs. All the songs have been carefully graded into an easy-to-follow, lesson-by-lesson format, which assumes no prior knowledge of music or the piano by the student.

Method Book 3 introduces five chords in the left hand (C, G7, F, G and D7) and three new notes in the right hand (D, F♯ and B♭). More challenging accompaniments are provided to help students develop their ability to co-ordinate their left and right hands, as well as offering practice in the art of reading popular sheet music. The book also explains how to change between chords efficiently, as well as discussing the left and right hand G positions.

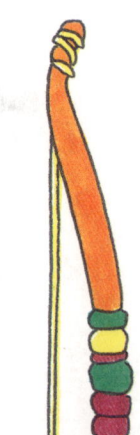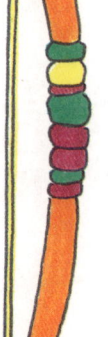

New pieces of information are highlighted by color boxes, and color illustrations are used throughout to stimulate and maintain the student's interest.

Supplementary Songbook C contains an additional 29 songs which are cross-referenced to the lessons in Method Book 3.

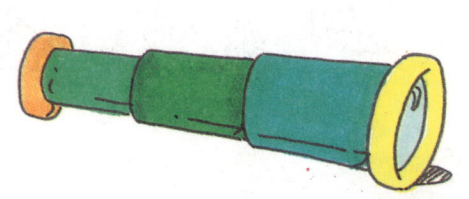

Lesson 1
Chords

A **chord** is a group of notes which are played together. Chords are used to play along with the melody of a song. The first chord you will learn is the C major chord, usually just called the C chord.

The C Chord

The C chord contains three notes – C, E and G. To play the C chord, use the **first**, **third** and **fifth** fingers of your left hand, as shown in the C chord diagram.

1  Careful Canary

Chord symbols are written above each bar to remind you of the name of the chord you are playing.

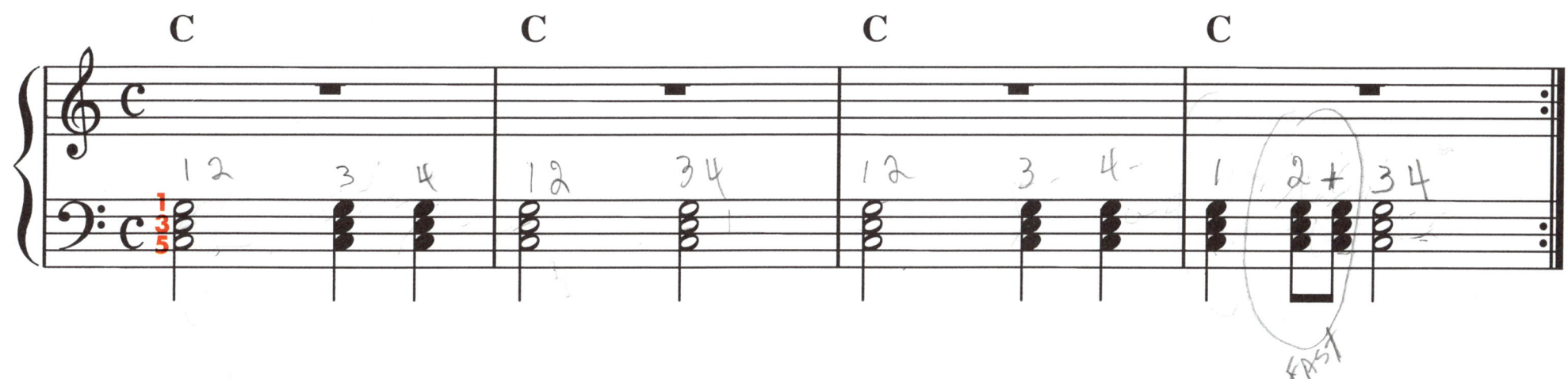

Seventh Chords

Another type of chord you can play is called a **seventh** chord. A seventh chord is indicated by the number 7 written after the chord name, for example G7.

The G Seventh Chord (G7)

The G7 chord contains a new note – the B next to the C below Middle C. Play the B with the **fifth** finger of your left hand, and use your **first** and **second** fingers to play the G and F notes, as shown in the G7 chord diagram.

2 Vanilla Gorilla

Changing Chords

Practice changing between the C and G7 chords. Because there is a G note in each chord, you can keep your thumb on it as you change from the C chord to G7. You can also keep your thumb on the G note when changing back from the G7 chord to C. This will make changing chords very easy.

3 **Two Chord Tango**

Practice changing between the C and G7 chords in this song.

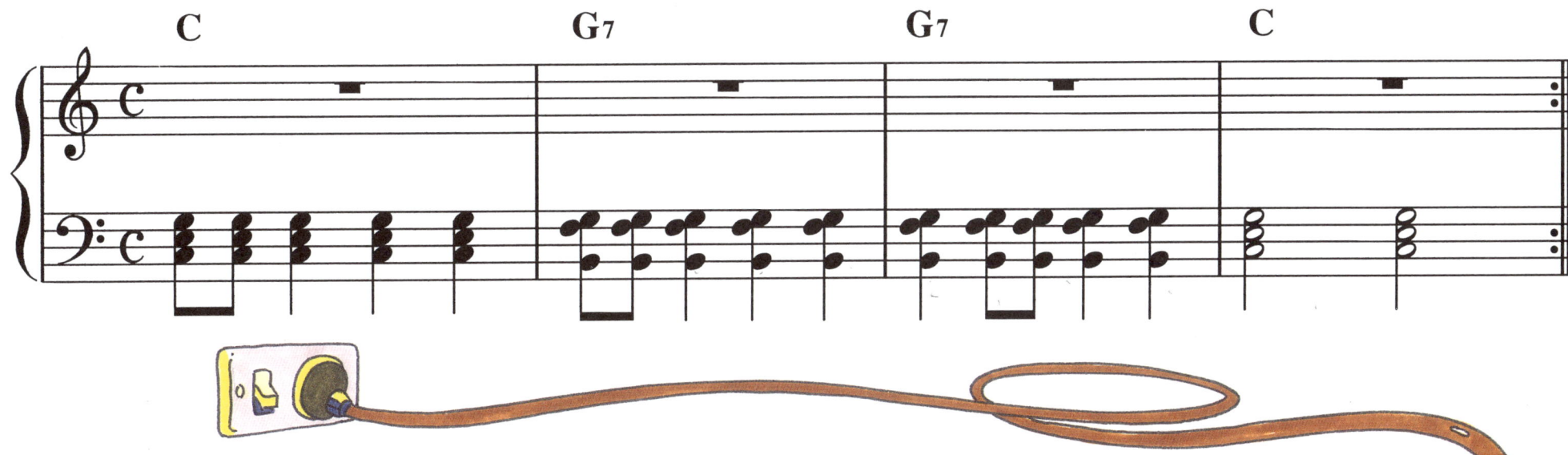

 You can now play the songs on page 5 of Supplementary Songbook C.

Lesson 2
Songs with Chords

Before playing songs with chords, practice each part separately. First practice the melody of the song by itself (right hand part), then practice the chords by themselves (left hand part). Once you have learnt both parts, play them together. Practice slowly and evenly, and count as you play. The part containing the chords is sometimes called the **accompaniment**.

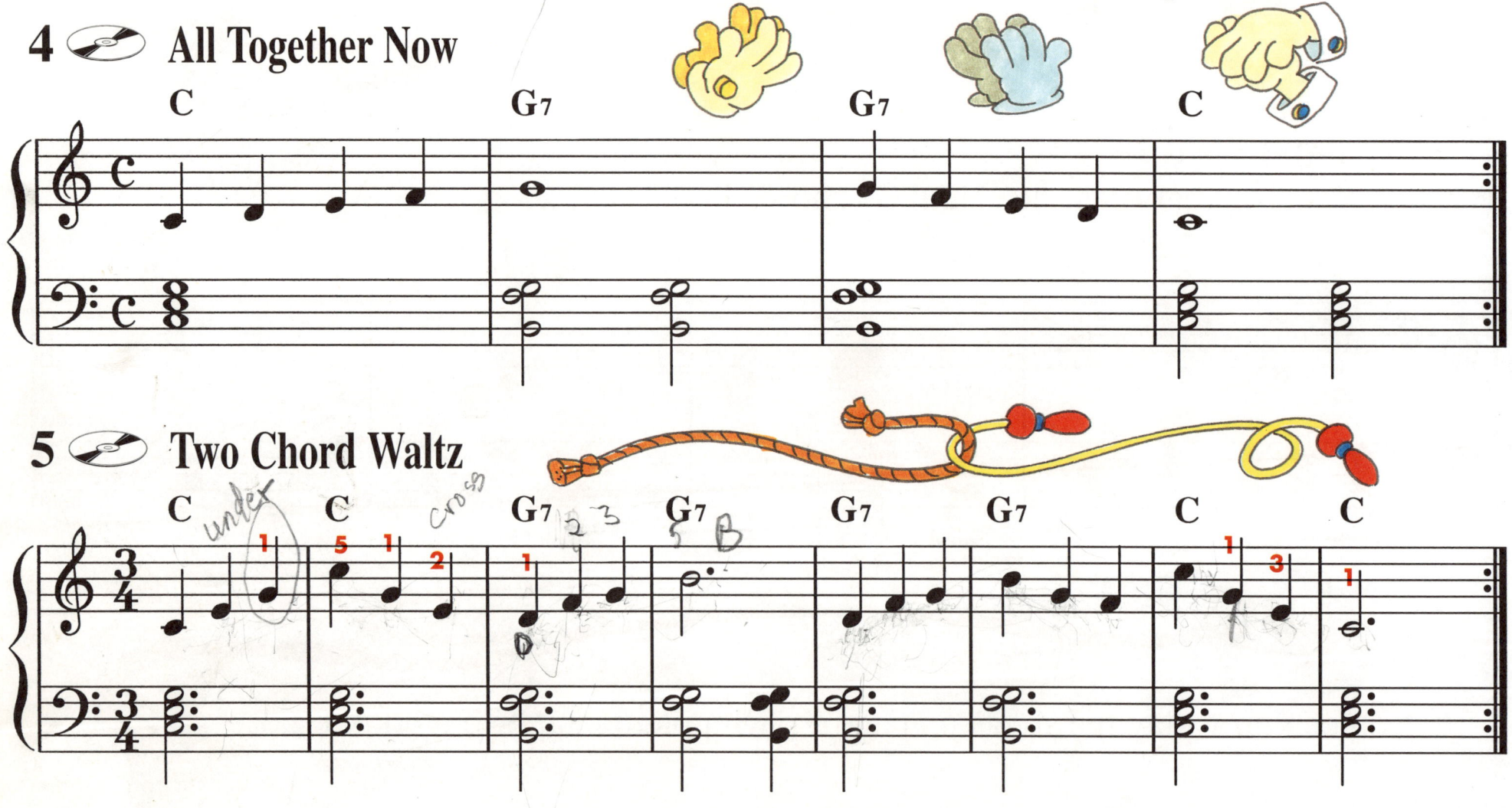

4. All Together Now

5. Two Chord Waltz

7 Buffalo Gals

Traditional

On the recording there are **three** beats to introduce this song.

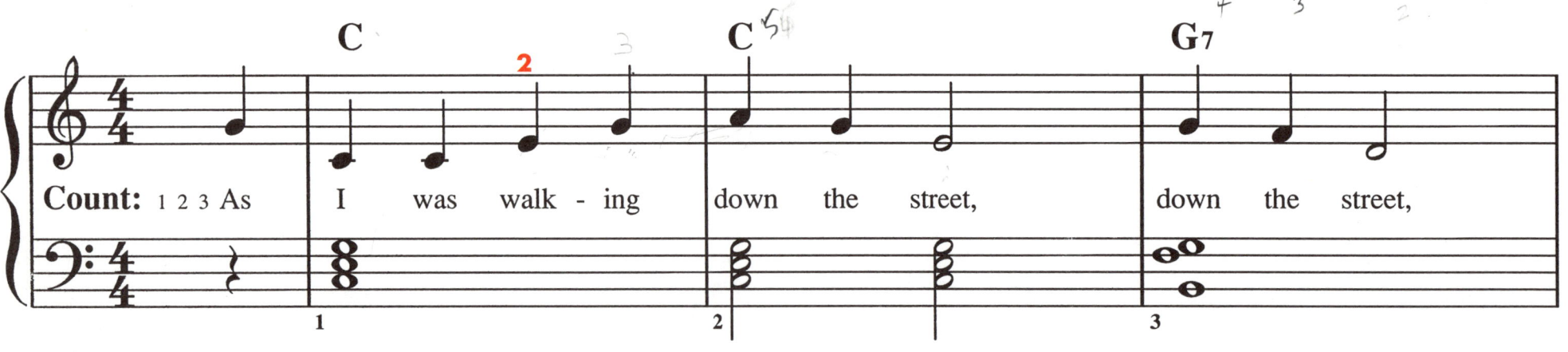
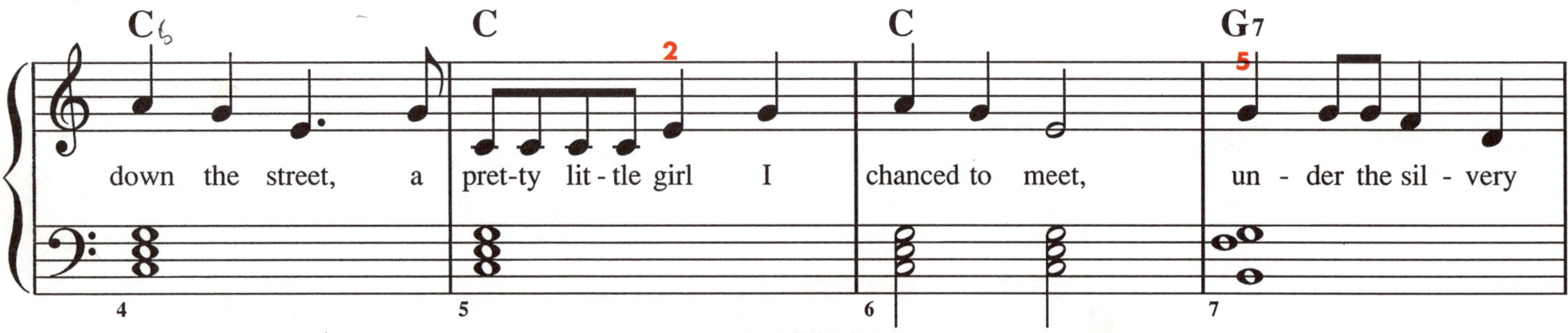

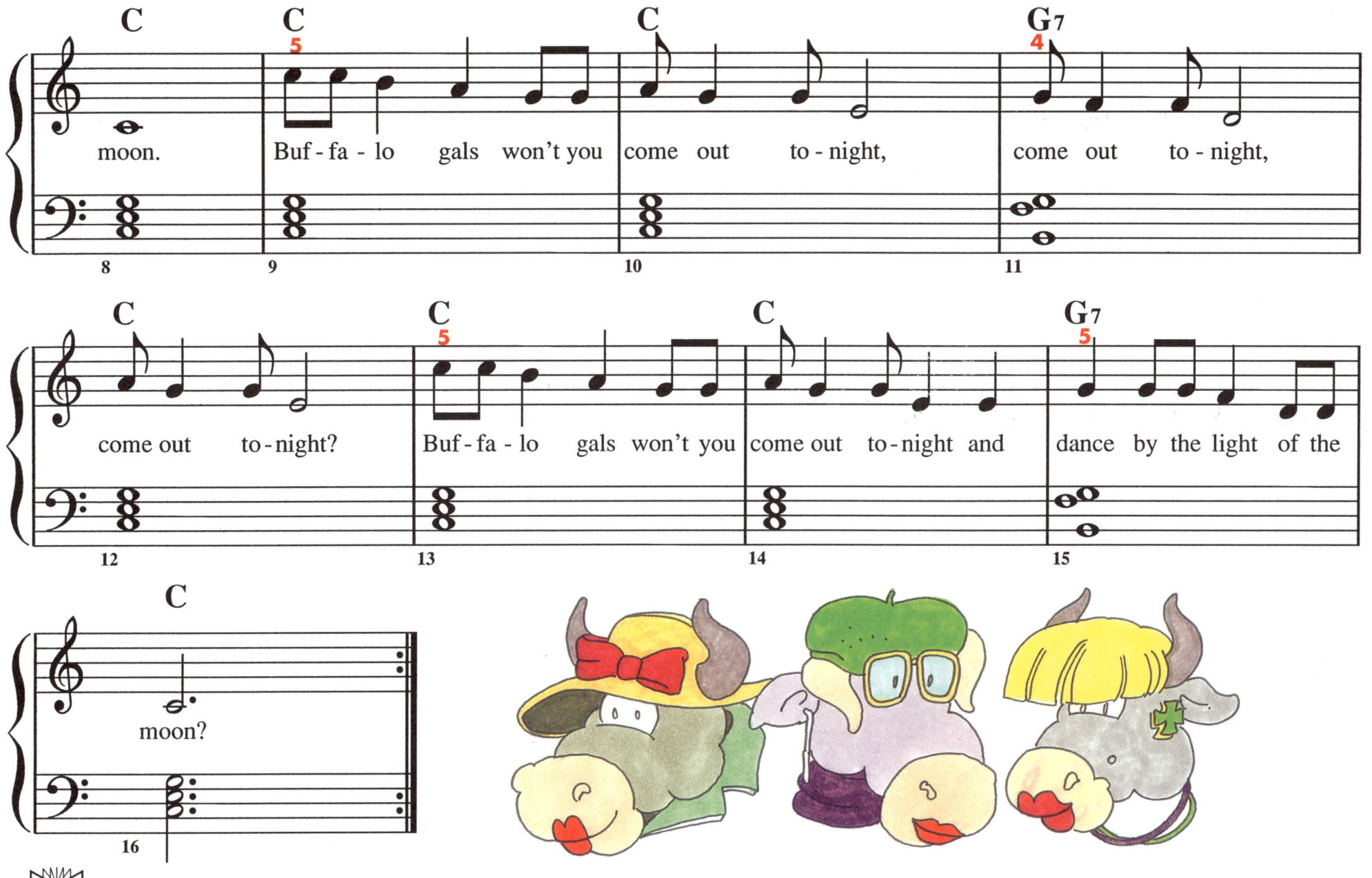

You can now play the songs on page 6 to 11 of Supplementary Songbook C.

Lesson 3
The F Chord

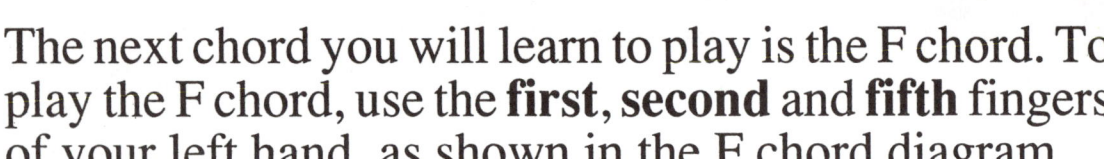

The next chord you will learn to play is the F chord. To play the F chord, use the **first**, **second** and **fifth** fingers of your left hand, as shown in the F chord diagram.

Gone Fishing

Changing between C and F

The song Something Fishy has two chords, the C chord and the F chord. As there is a C note in both chords, you can keep your fifth finger on it when you change between them. This will make changing chords very easy.

Something Fishy

10 On Top of Old Smoky

Traditional

This song contains all three chords you have learnt so far. Remember to keep your fifth finger on the C key when changing between C and F, and your thumb on the G key when changing between C and G7.

On the recording there are **five** beats to introduce this song.

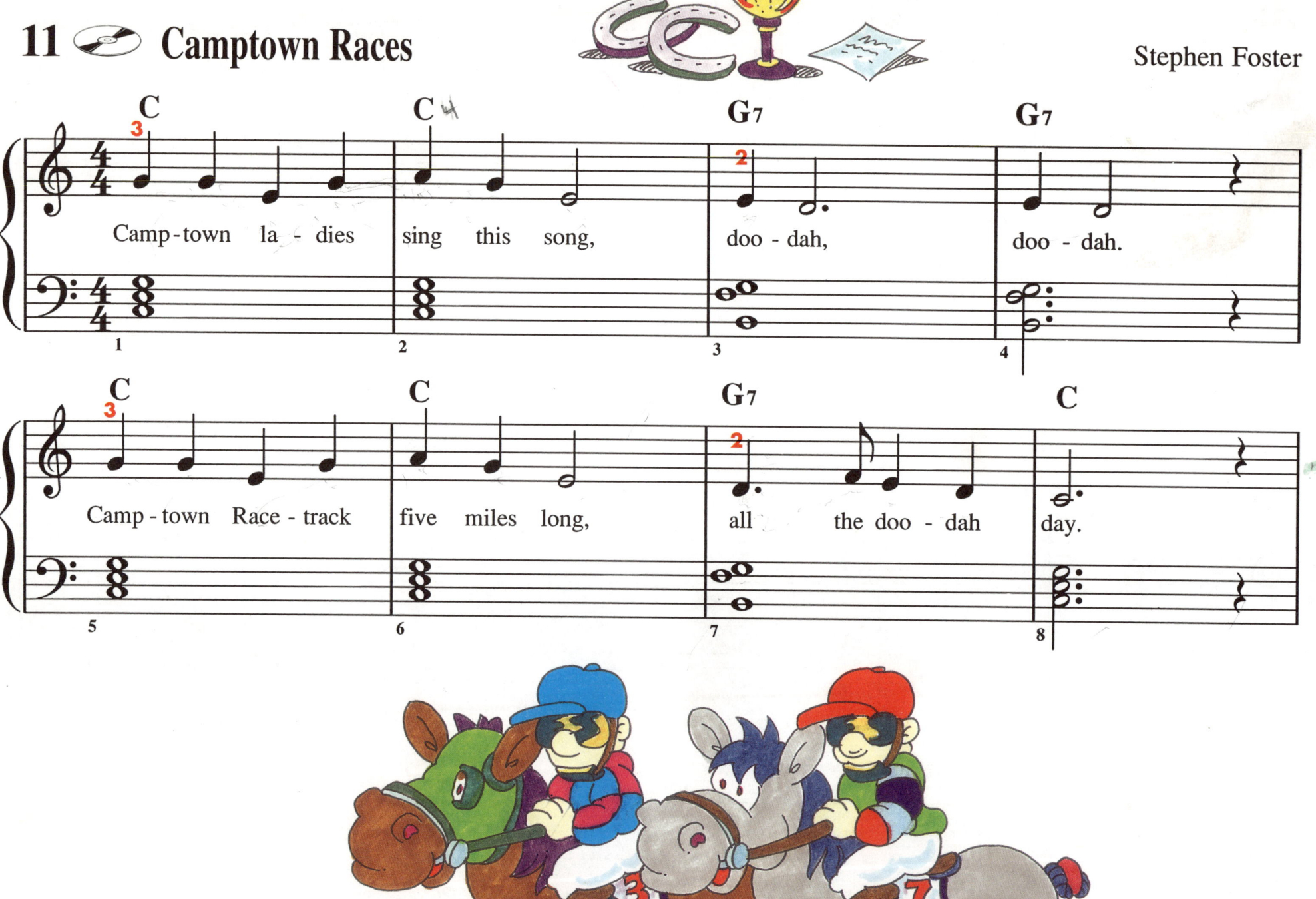

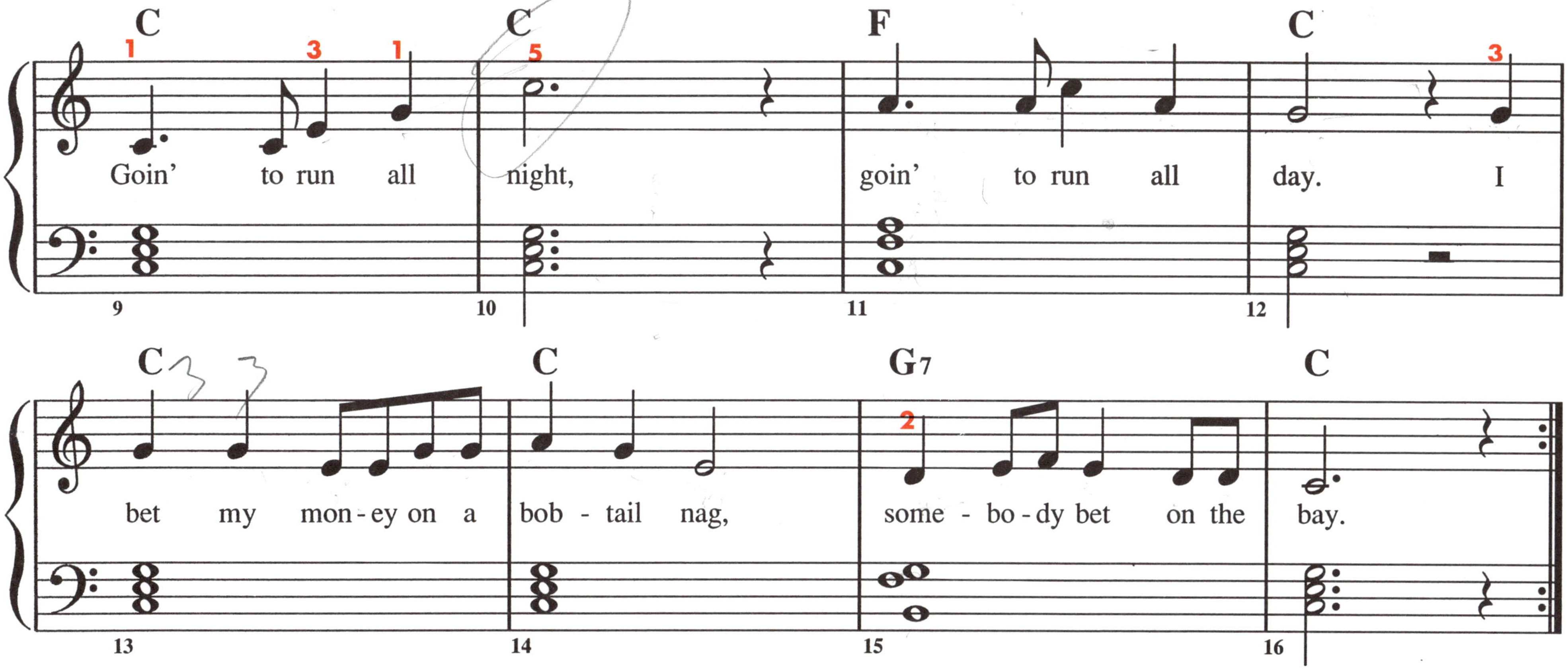

You can now play the songs on pages 12 to 15 of Supplementary Songbook C.

Sharp Signs

 This is a **sharp** sign.

When a sharp sign is placed before a note on the staff, it means that you play the key immediately to its right. This key may be either **black** or **white**. The note F sharp below Middle C (written as F#) is shown on the staff below.

The Note F# (F Sharp) On the Bass Staff

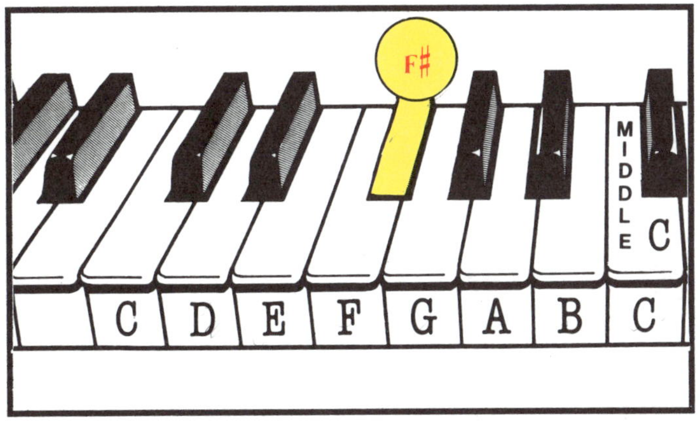

To play the note F#, play the **black** key immediately to the right of the F note as shown in the diagram.

13 Sharp Turn

The D7 Chord

To play the D7 chord use the **first**, **second** and **fifth** fingers of your left hand, as shown in the D7 diagram.

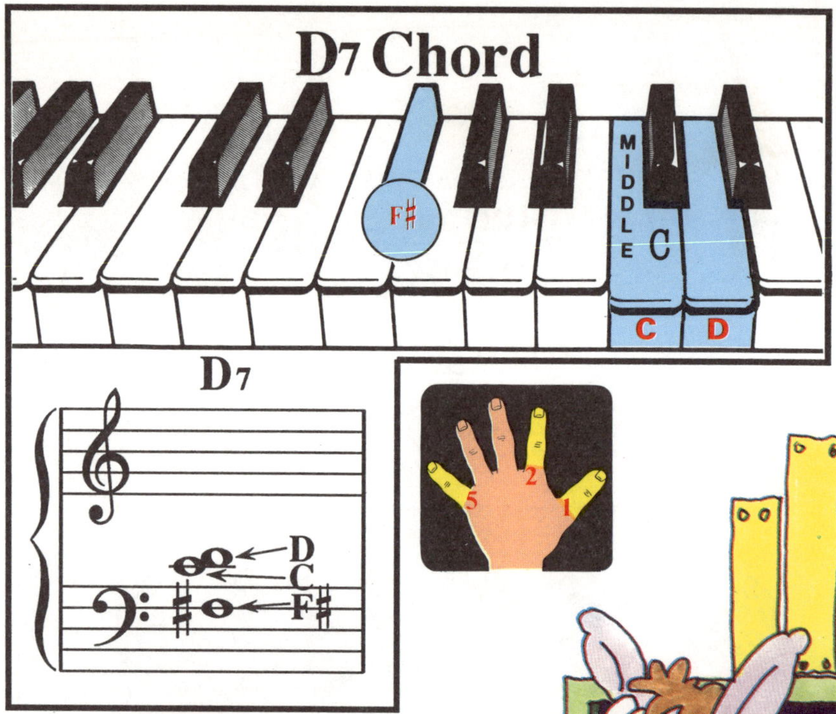

14 Donkey Dance

When a sharp sign is written before an F note, it applies to all F notes which come after the sign in that bar. Thus, bars 1 and 2 both contain three F# notes each.

Changing between G and D7

The next song has two chords, the C chord and the D7 chord. As there is a D note in both chords, you can keep your thumb on it when you change between the chords. This will make changing between G and D7 very easy.

15 Seven Drowsy Donkeys

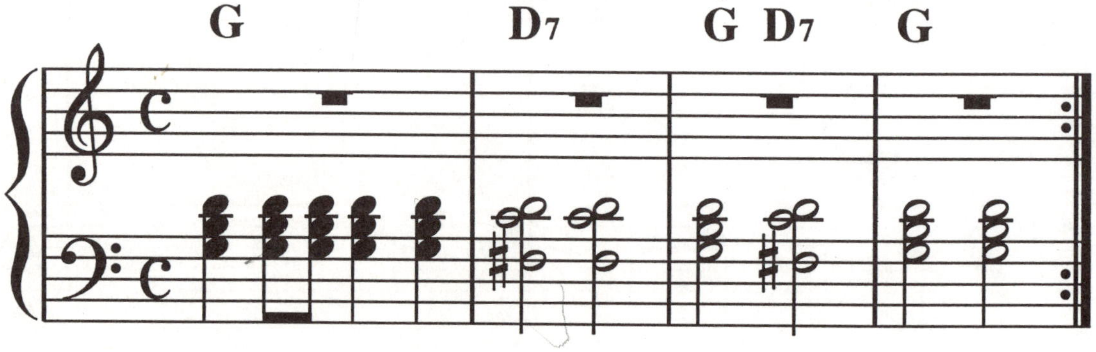

16 🔘 How Dry I Am

Traditional

Instead of writing a sharp sign before every F note on the staff, it is easier to write just one sharp sign after each clef. This means that all the F notes on the staff are played as F#, even though there is no sharp sign written before them.

On the recording there are **five** beats to introduce this song.

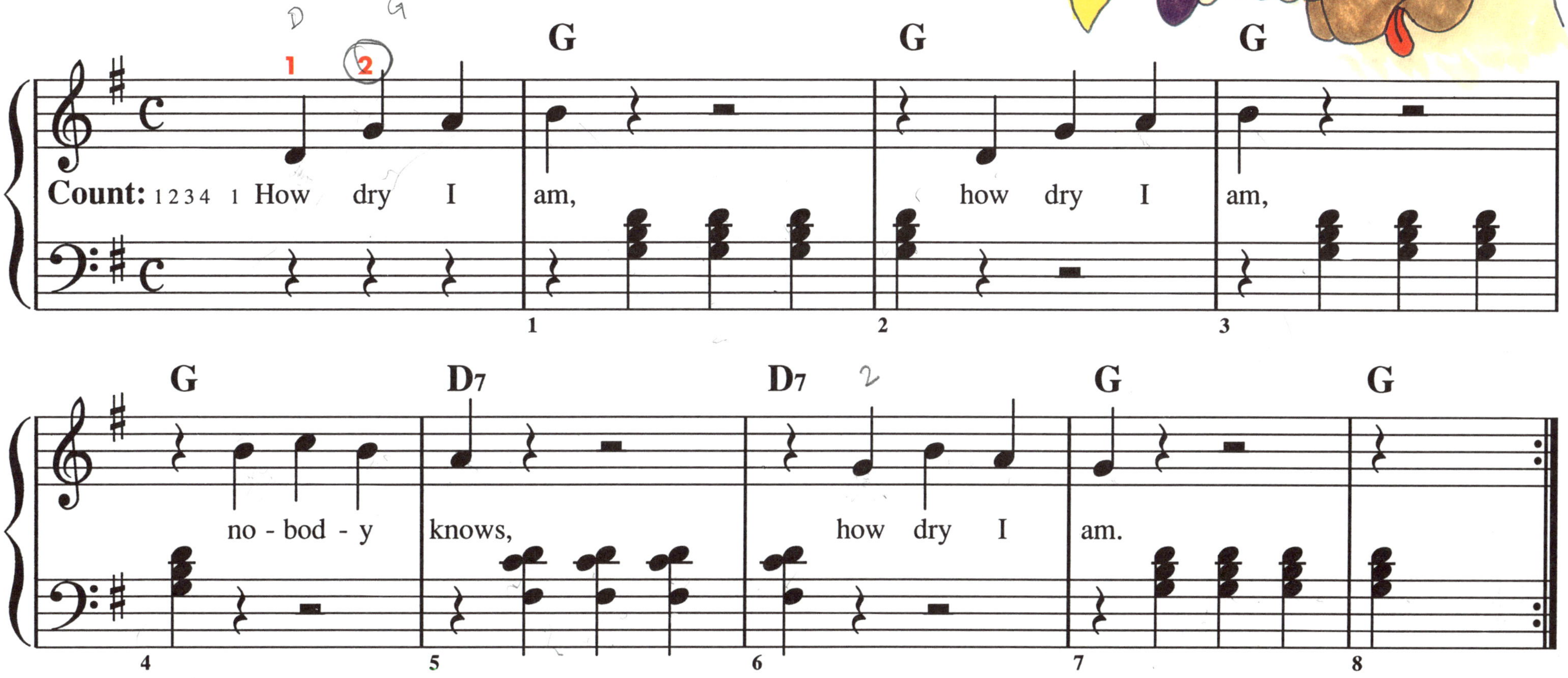

 You can now play the song Paper of Pins on page 16 of Supplementary Songbook C.

You can now play the song English Country Gardens on page 18 of Supplementary Songbook C.

The G Position

In Lessons 9 and 12 of Book 2, you learnt the C and F hand positions. In this lesson you will learn the G position, which you should use when you play songs which contain the G and D_7 chords.

Left Hand G Position

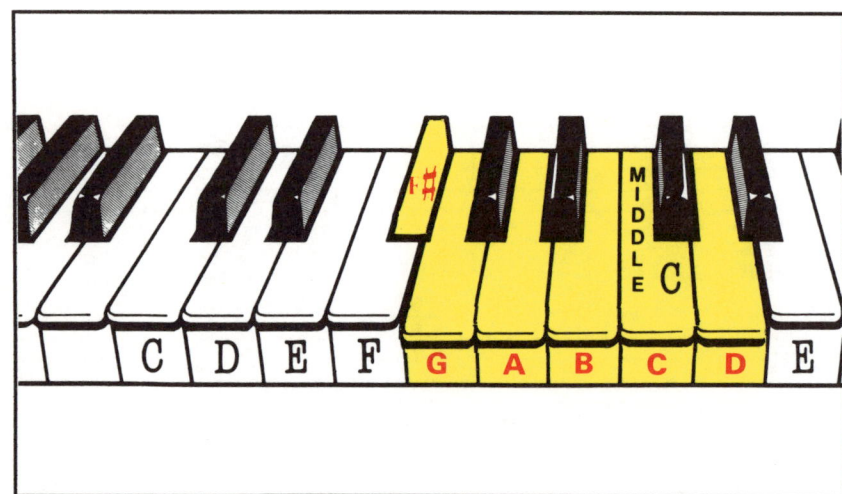

The left hand G position covers the notes from F♯ up to D.

Right Hand G Position

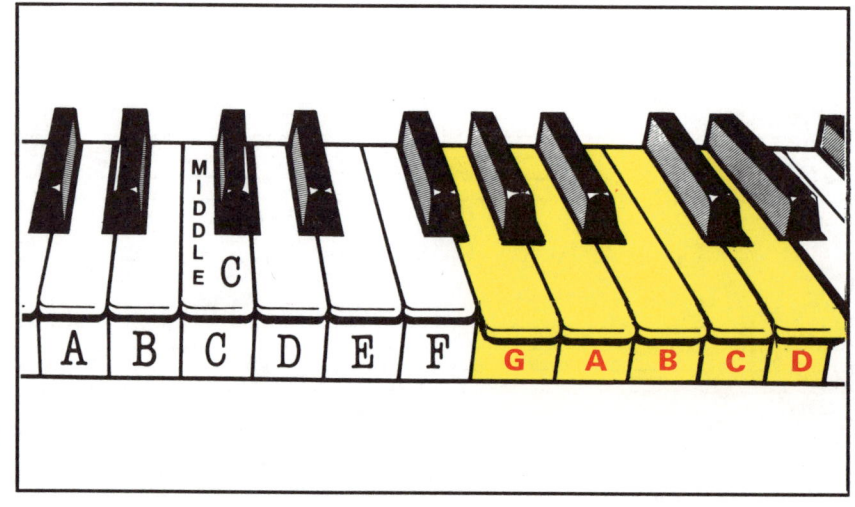

The right hand G position covers the notes from G up to D.

The song Lightly Row, on page 20, is played in the G position.

Lesson 6
The Note F♯
(on the Treble Staff)

This F♯ note is written in the second space of the treble staff.

On page 19, you learnt that a sharp sign written after the bass clef at the start of a line applies to all F notes on the bass staff. Similarly, when a sharp sign is written after the treble clef, it applies to all F notes on the treble staff.

19. Two Sharp

This song contains two F♯ notes on the treble staff – one each in bars 1 and 3.

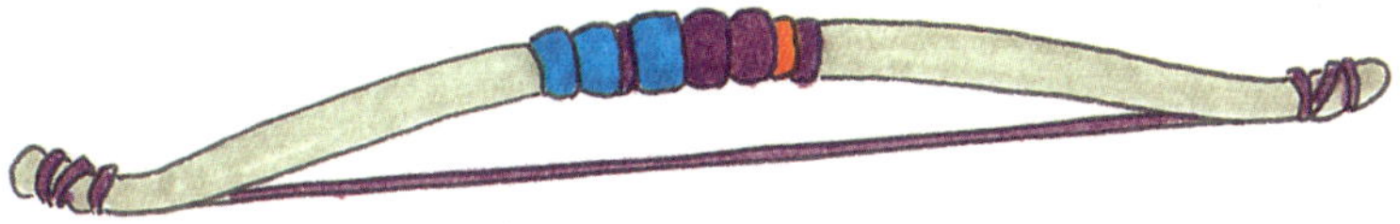

Playing Parts of Chords

Sometimes an accompaniment may use only one or two notes of a chord, instead of three notes. For example, in the next song, The William Tell Overture, there are six bars on the bass staff which only use the two lowest notes of the chord. Pay close attention to the notes written on the bass staff.

20 🎧 **The William Tell Overture**   Giaochino Rossini

On the recording there are **three** beats to introduce this song.

21 Ten Little Indians

Traditional

One lit-tle two lit-tle three lit-tle In-di-ans, four lit-tle five lit-tle six lit-tle In-di-ans, seven lit-tle eight lit-tle nine lit-tle In-di-ans, ten lit-tle In-di-an boys.

You can now play the song Rock-a-bye Baby, on page 20 of Supplementary Songbook C.

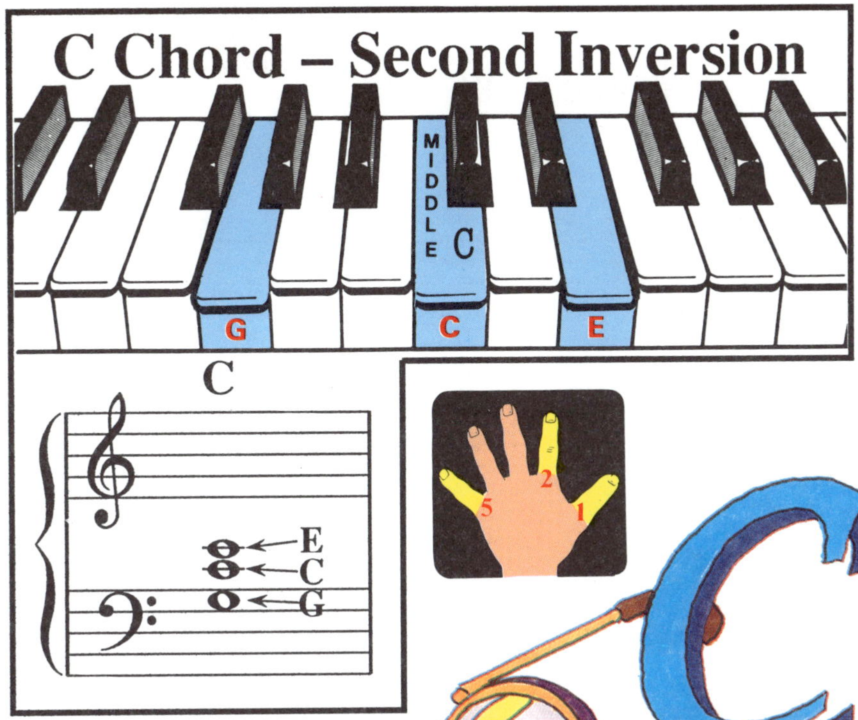

Lesson 7
Another Fingering for the C Chord

C Chord – Second Inversion

22 C What I Mean

In Lesson 1, you learnt that the C chord contains three notes – C, E and G – and you learnt how to play the C chord with the C as the lowest note of the chord. Sometimes it is easier to play the C chord with G as the lowest note. To play the C chord in this way, use the **first**, **second** and **fifth** fingers of your left hand, as shown in the diagram.

When C is the lowest note of the C chord, the chord is said to be in **root position**. When E is the lowest note, the chord is said to be in its **first inversion**. The new C chord fingering shown on this page, with G as the lowest note, is called the **second inversion** of the C chord.

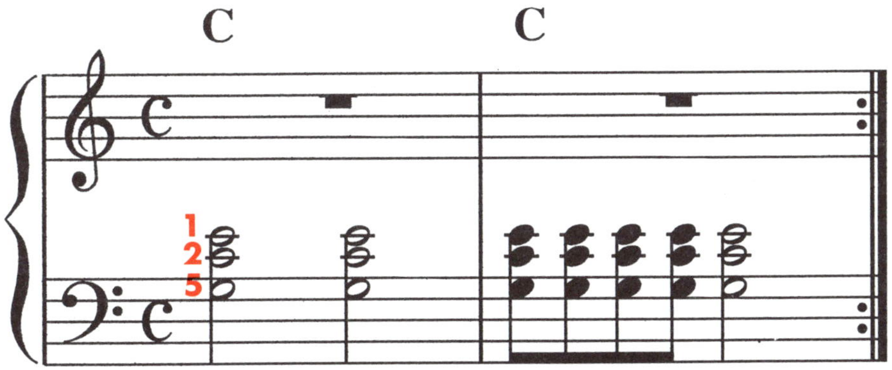

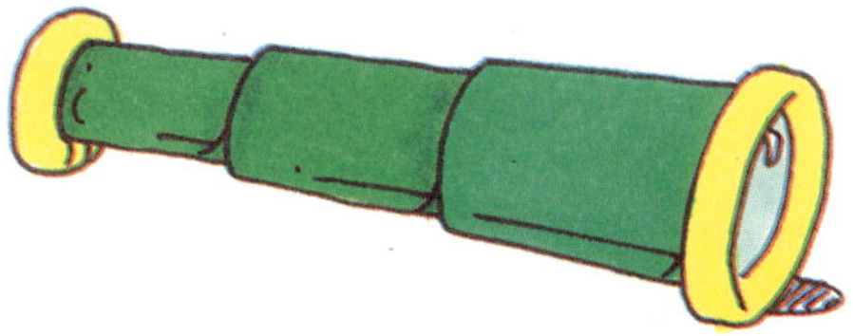

Changing between G and C

The next song has two chords, the G chord and the second inversion of the C chord. As there is a G note in both chords, you can keep your fifth finger on it when you change between them. This will make changing between G and C very easy.

23 Spare Change

24 Beautiful Brown Eyes

Traditional

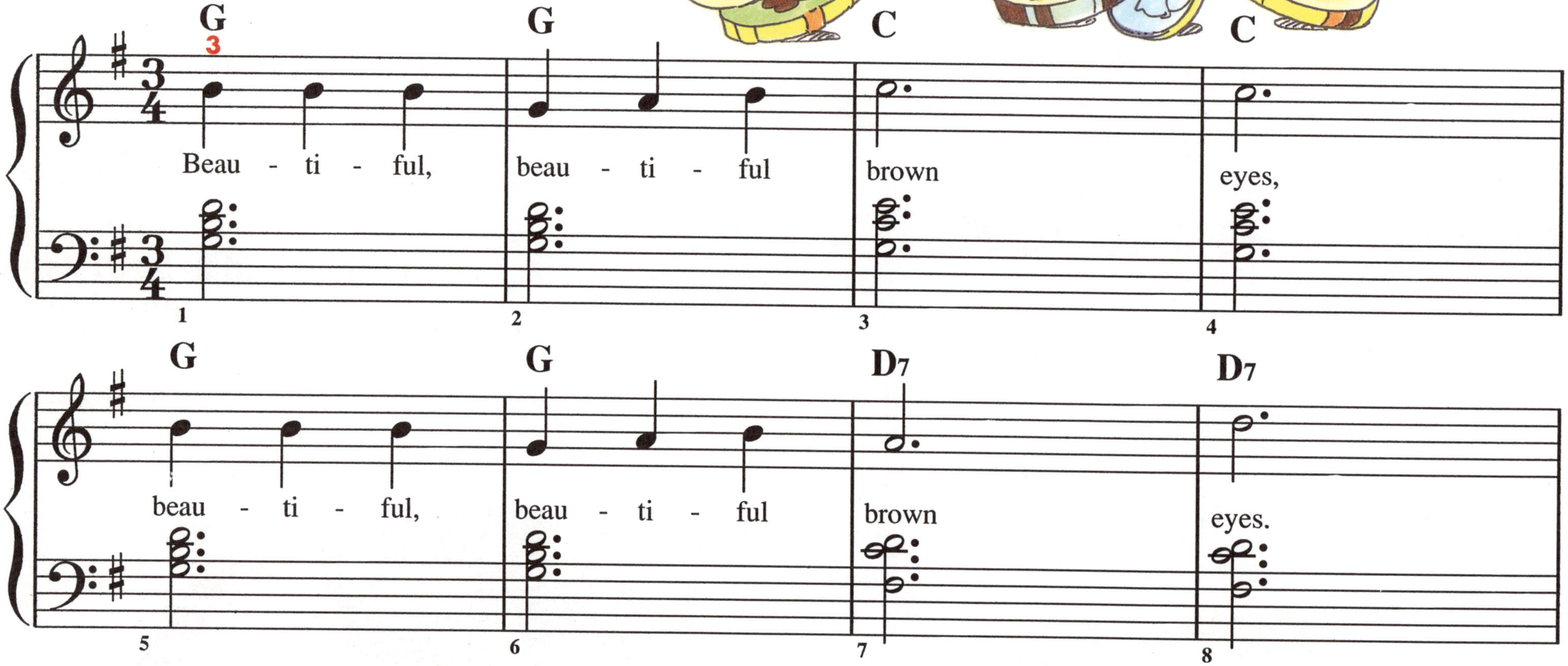

Beau - ti - ful, beau - ti - ful brown eyes,

beau - ti - ful, beau - ti - ful brown eyes.

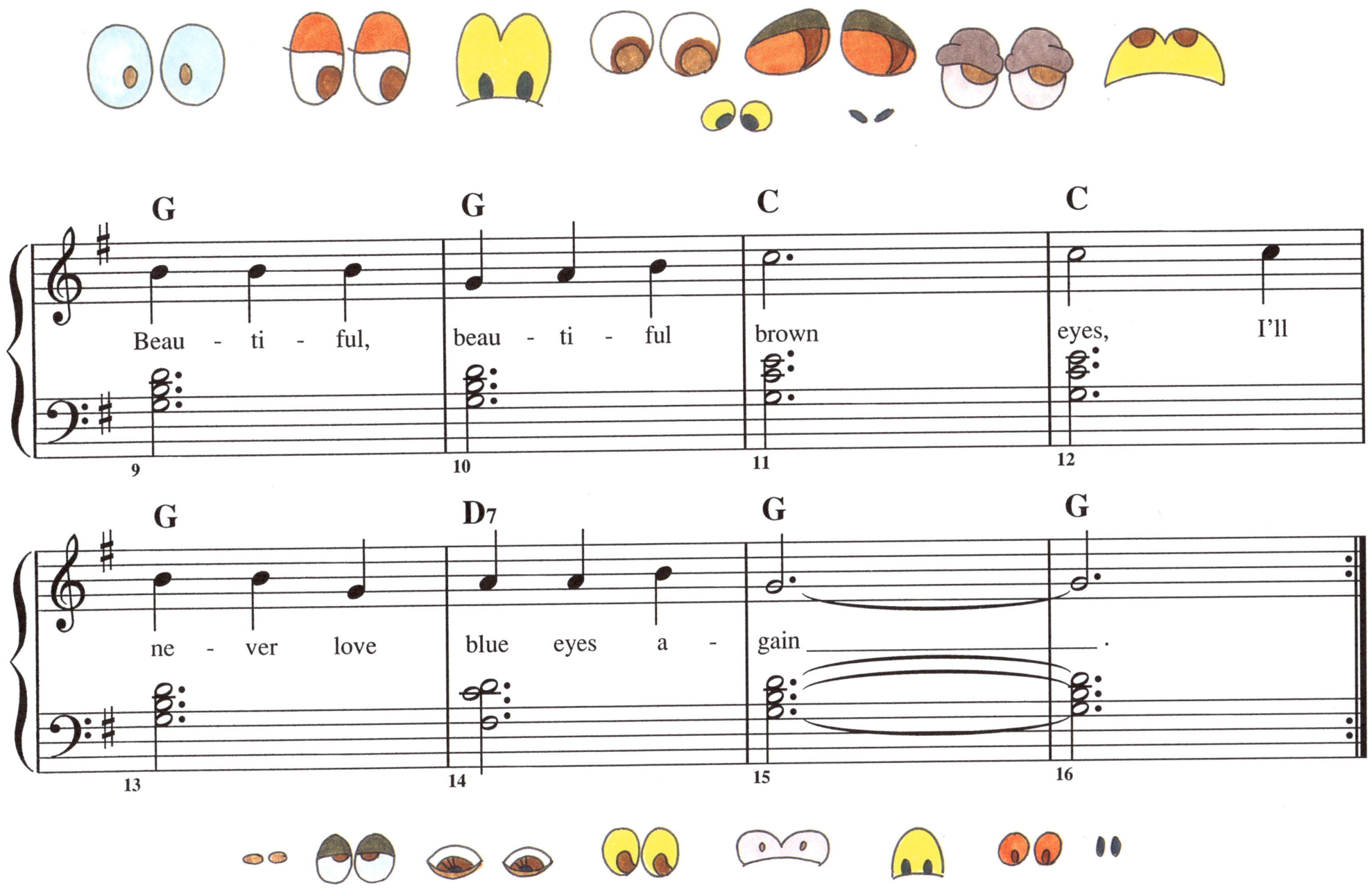

Lesson 8
The D7 Chord
(Another Fingering)

In Lesson 4, you learnt to play the D7 chord using the F#, C and D notes. Here is a different way of playing D7 which uses the A, C and D notes. To play D7 in this way, use the **first**, **second** and **fourth** fingers of your left hand.

25 Aloha Oe

This song contains the new D7 fingering in bars 5 and 13. On the recording there are **three** beats to introduce this song.

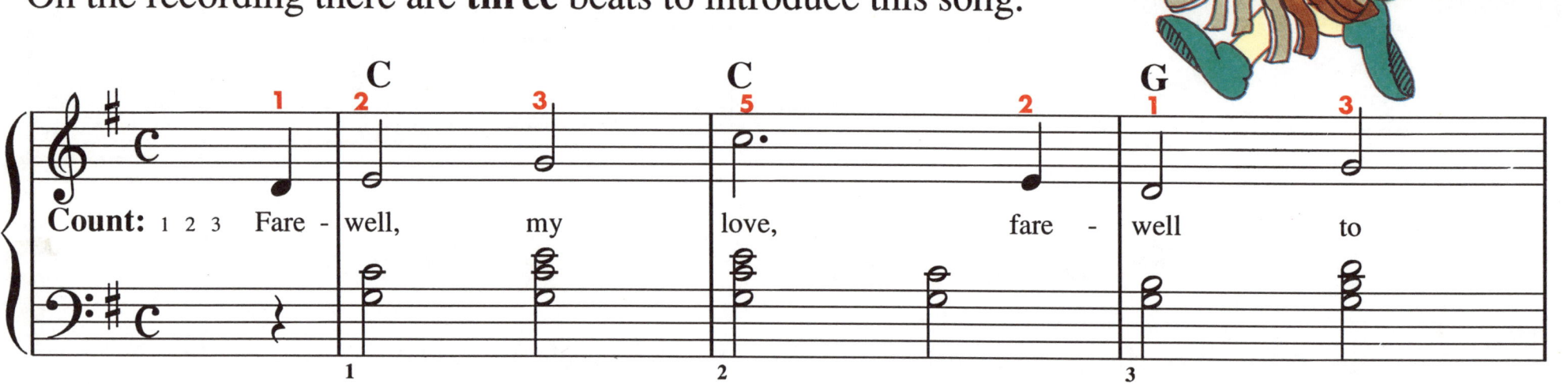

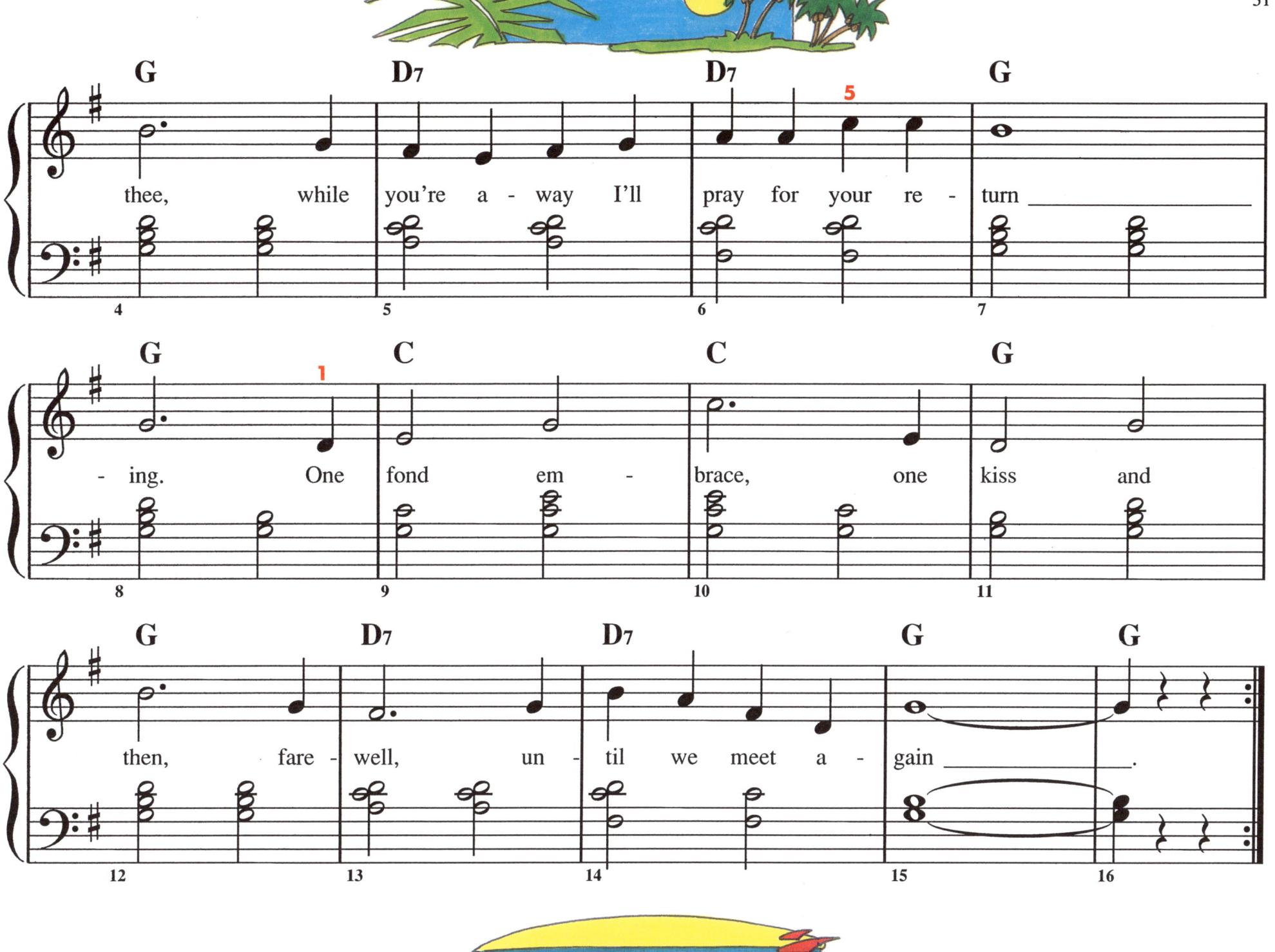

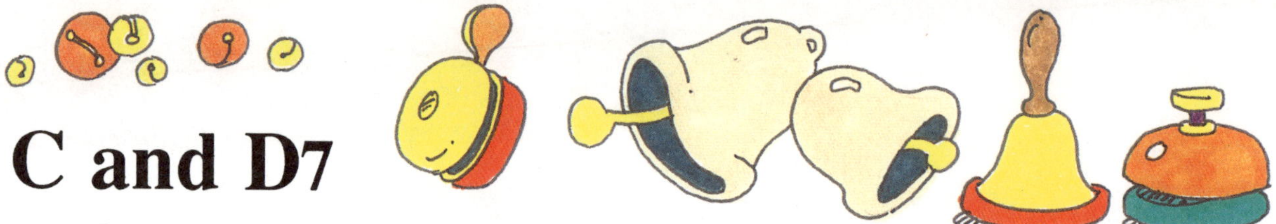

Changing between C and D7

In bars 3 and 9 of the next song there is a C chord followed by a D7 chord. As there is a C note in both chords, keep your second finger on it when you change between the chords.

26 Ding Dong Merrily on High

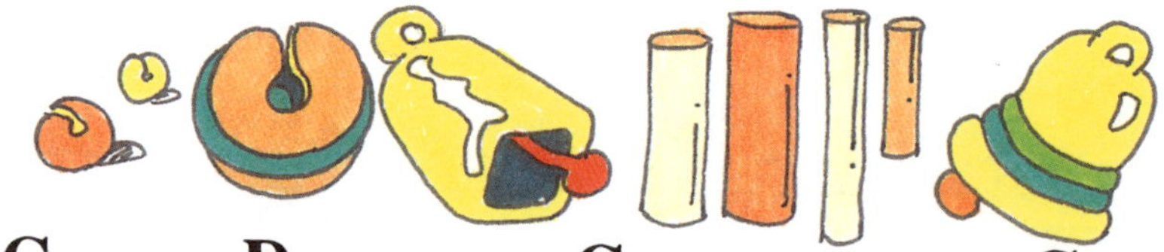

Traditional

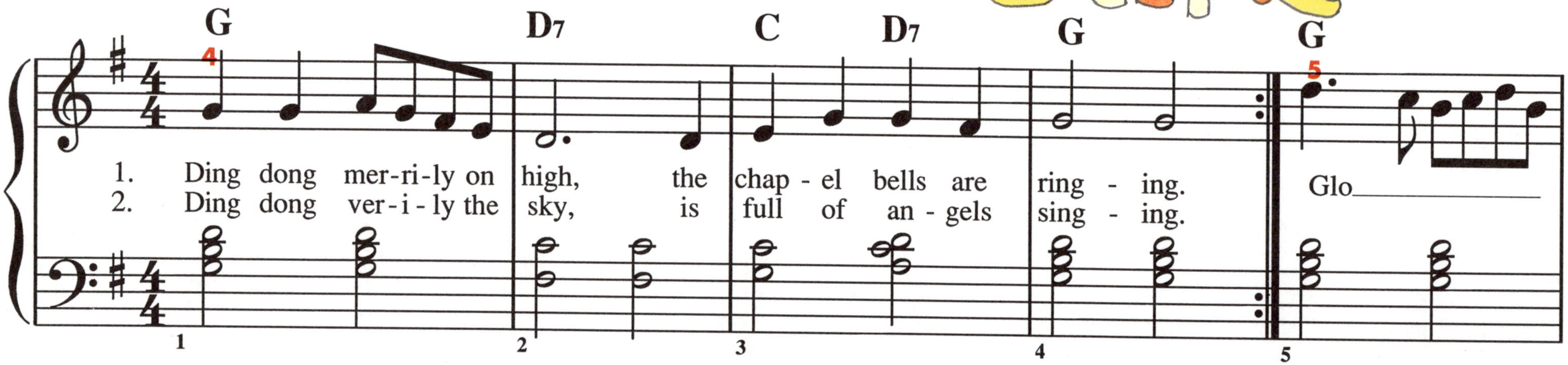
G
D7
C
D7
G
G
4
5
1. Ding dong mer-ri-ly on high, the chap - el bells are ring - ing.
2. Ding dong ver - i - ly the sky, is full of an - gels sing - ing.
Glo
1
2
3
4
5

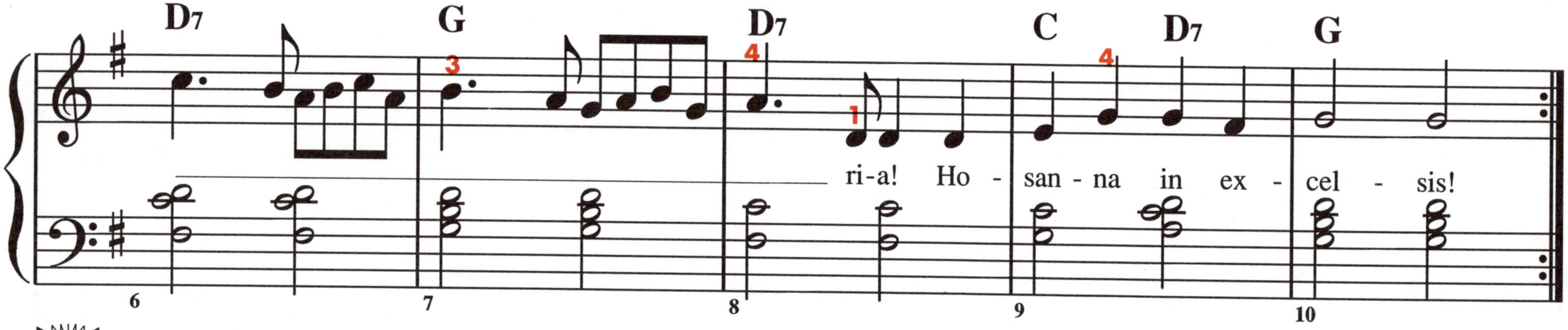
D7
G
D7
C
D7
G
3
4
1
4
ri - a! Ho - san - na in ex - cel - sis!
6
7
8
9
10

You can now play the songs on pages 28 to 35 of Supplementary Songbook C.

Lesson 9

Broken Chords

Sometimes when you play a chord, instead of playing all three notes together, you play the lowest note of the **chord shape** (chord fingering), followed by the other two notes of the chord.

27 C Saw

In this song, which is written in 4/4 time, the C chord is played as a broken chord. The lowest note of this C chord shape is C.

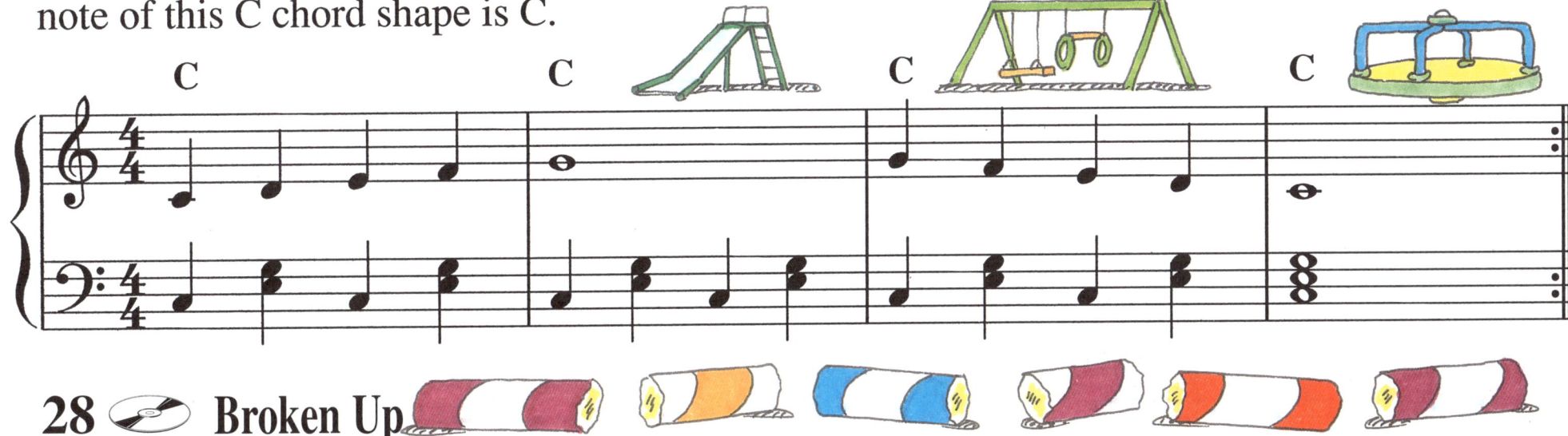

28 Broken Up

In this song, which is written in 3/4 time, the F chord is played as a broken chord. The lowest note of this F chord shape is C.

You can now play the songs on pages 36 to 39 of Supplementary Songbook C.

The G7 Chord
(Another Fingering)

In Lesson 1, you learnt to play the G7 chord using the B, F and G notes. Here is a different way of playing G7 which uses the D, F and G notes. To play this new G7 chord shape, use the **first**, **second** and **fourth** fingers of your left hand.

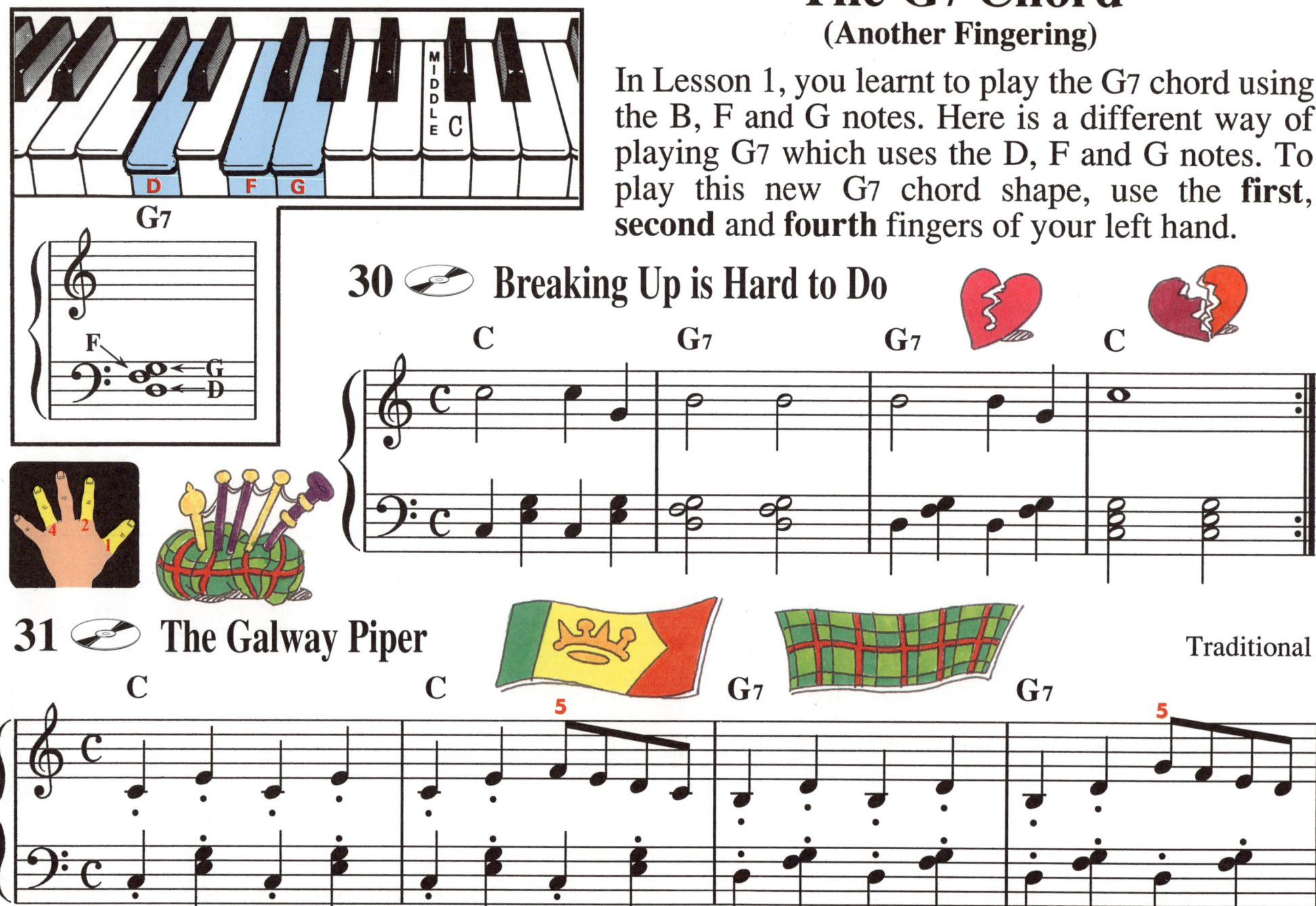

You can now play the song Sweet Betsy from Pike on pg 40 of Supplementary Songbook C.

♭ This is a **flat** sign.

Lesson 10
Flat Signs

When a flat sign is placed before a note on the staff, it means that you play the key immediately to its left. This key may be either **black** or **white**. The note B flat (written as B♭) is shown on the staff below.

The Note B♭ (B Flat)

To play the note B♭ play the **black** key immediately to the left of the B note as shown in the diagram.

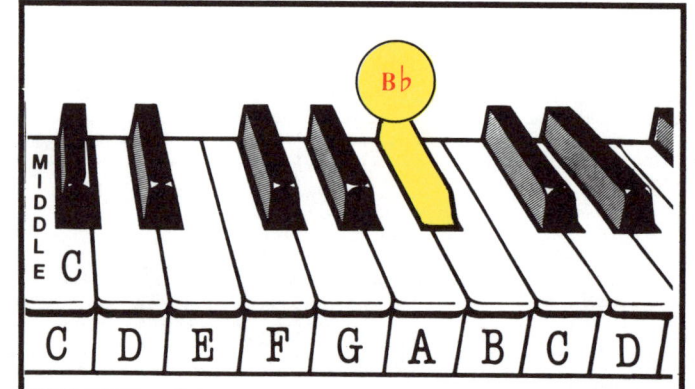

B♭ Note

32 🎵 **Bee Flat**

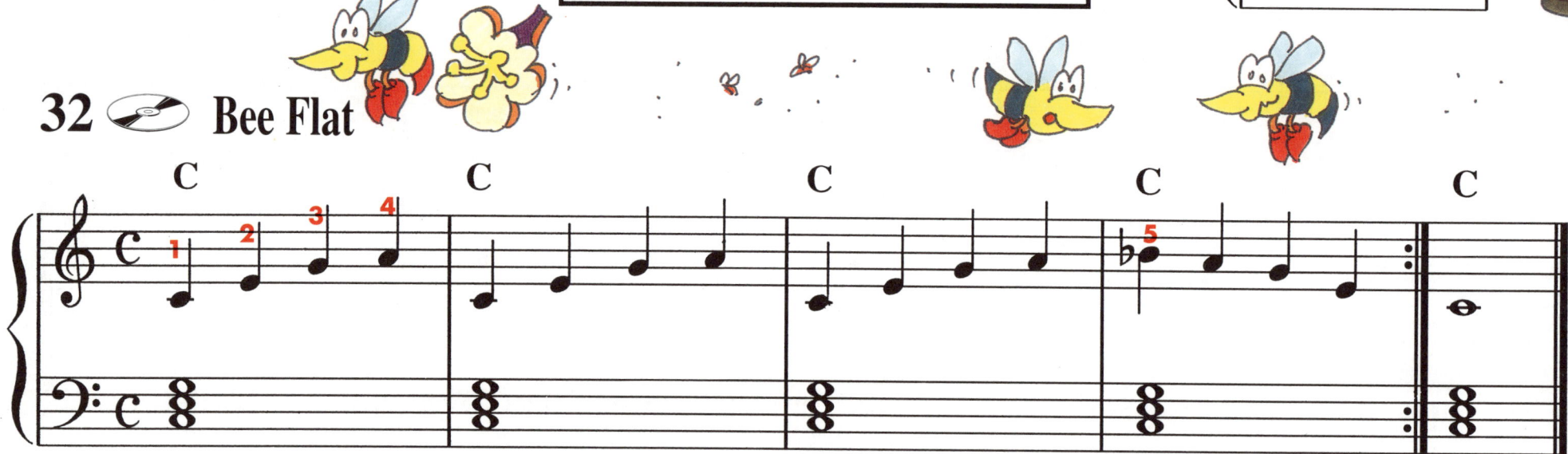

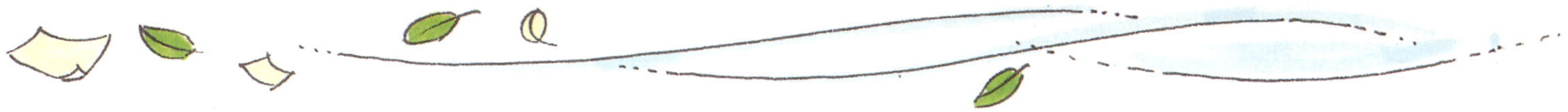

Instead of writing a flat sign before every B note on the staff, it is easier to write just one flat sign after each clef. This means that all the B notes on the staff are played as B♭, even though there is no flat sign written before them.

33 Blow the Man Down

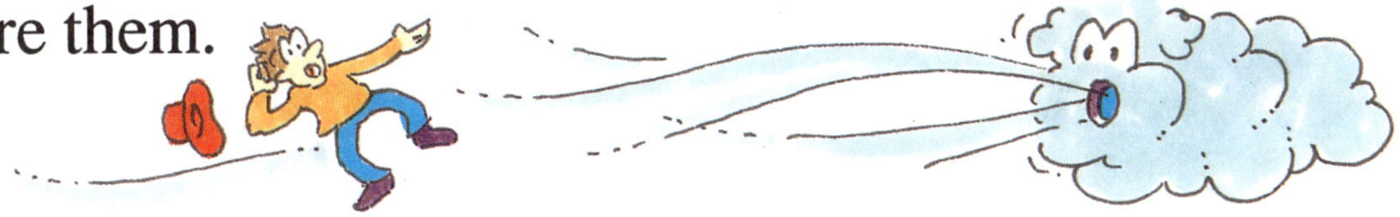

Traditional

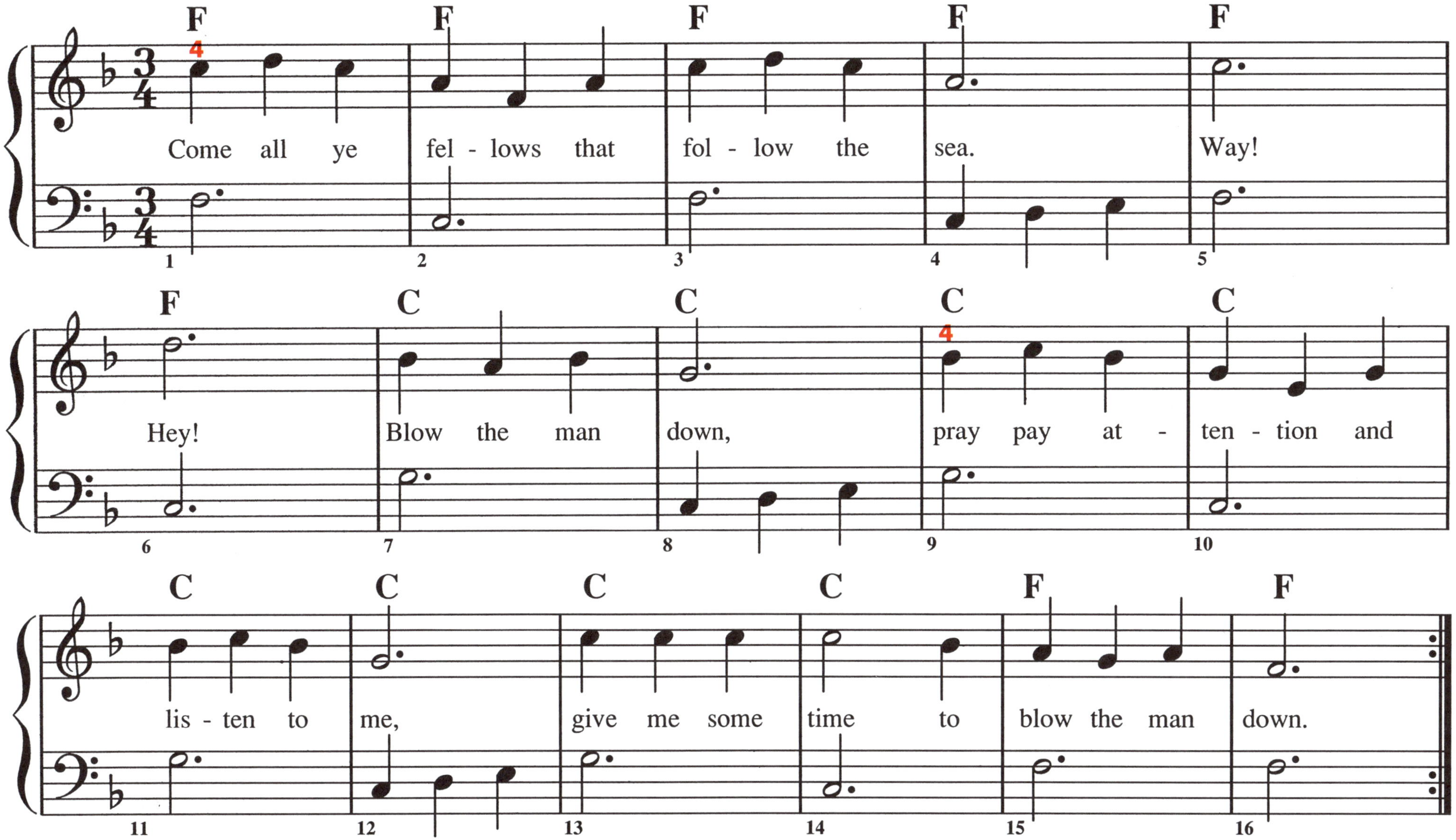
F F F F F
Come all ye fel - lows that fol - low the sea. Way!
1 2 3 4 5
F C C C C
Hey! Blow the man down, pray pay at - ten - tion and
6 7 8 9 10
C C C C F F
lis - ten to me, give me some time to blow the man down.
11 12 13 14 15 16

You can now play the songs on pages 42 to 45 of Supplementary Songbook C.

Lesson 11
The Note B♭
(below Middle C)

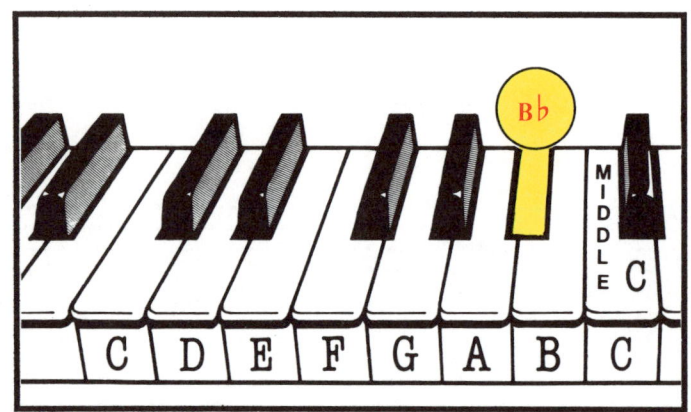

This B♭ note is written in the space above the bass staff.

34  **Blues For a Bee**

35 🎵 Go Round and Round the Village

Traditional English

On page 32 you learnt that a flat sign written on a line at the beginning of the treble staff applied to all notes on that line. The same rule applies to a flat sign written on the bass staff. Also, the flat sign on the second line of the bass staff applies to all B notes above the staff. Thus the 2nd note in bars 2, 3 and 6 is B♭ in each case.

On the recording there are **three** beats to introduce this song.

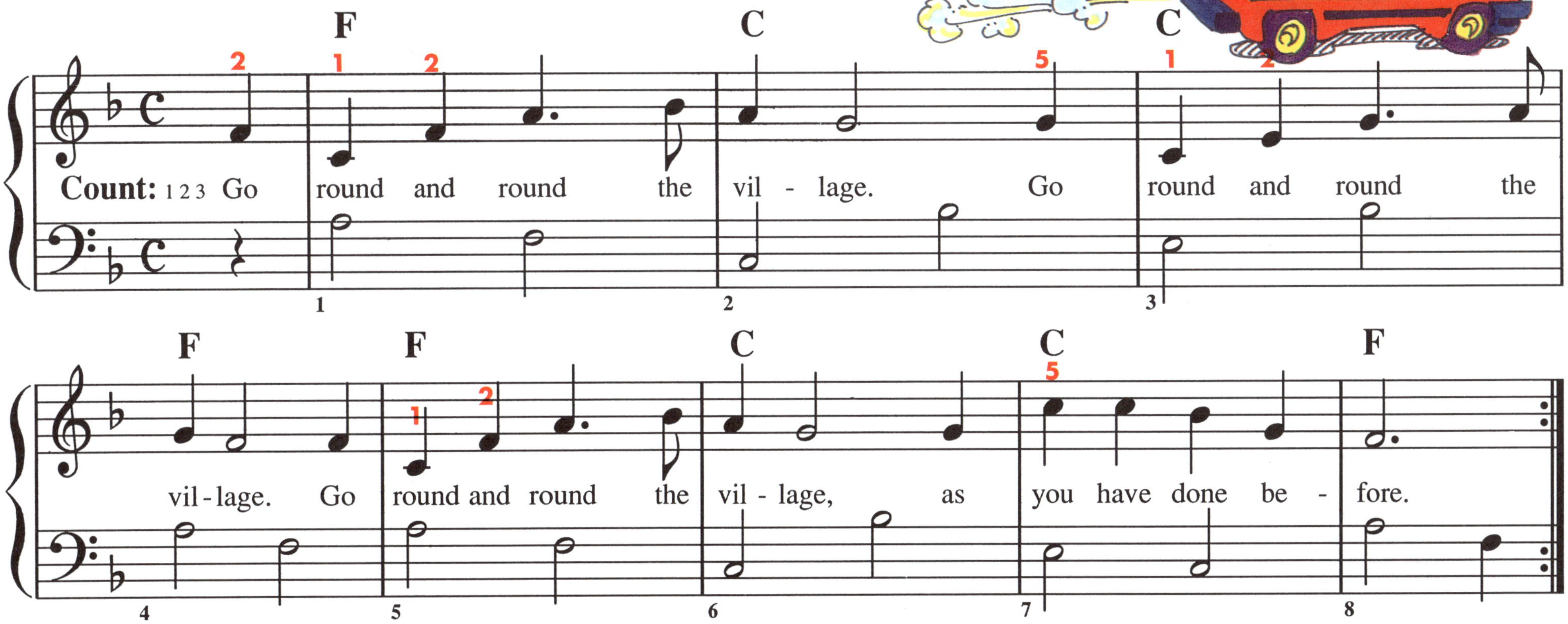

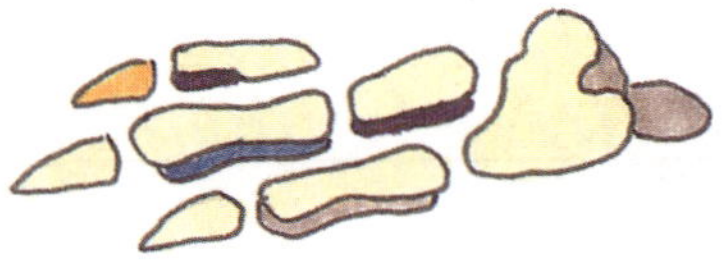

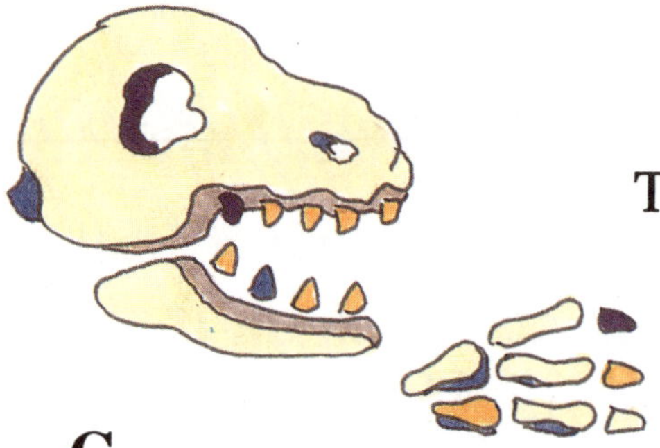

36 Dry Bones

Traditional

On the recording there are **three** beats to introduce this song.

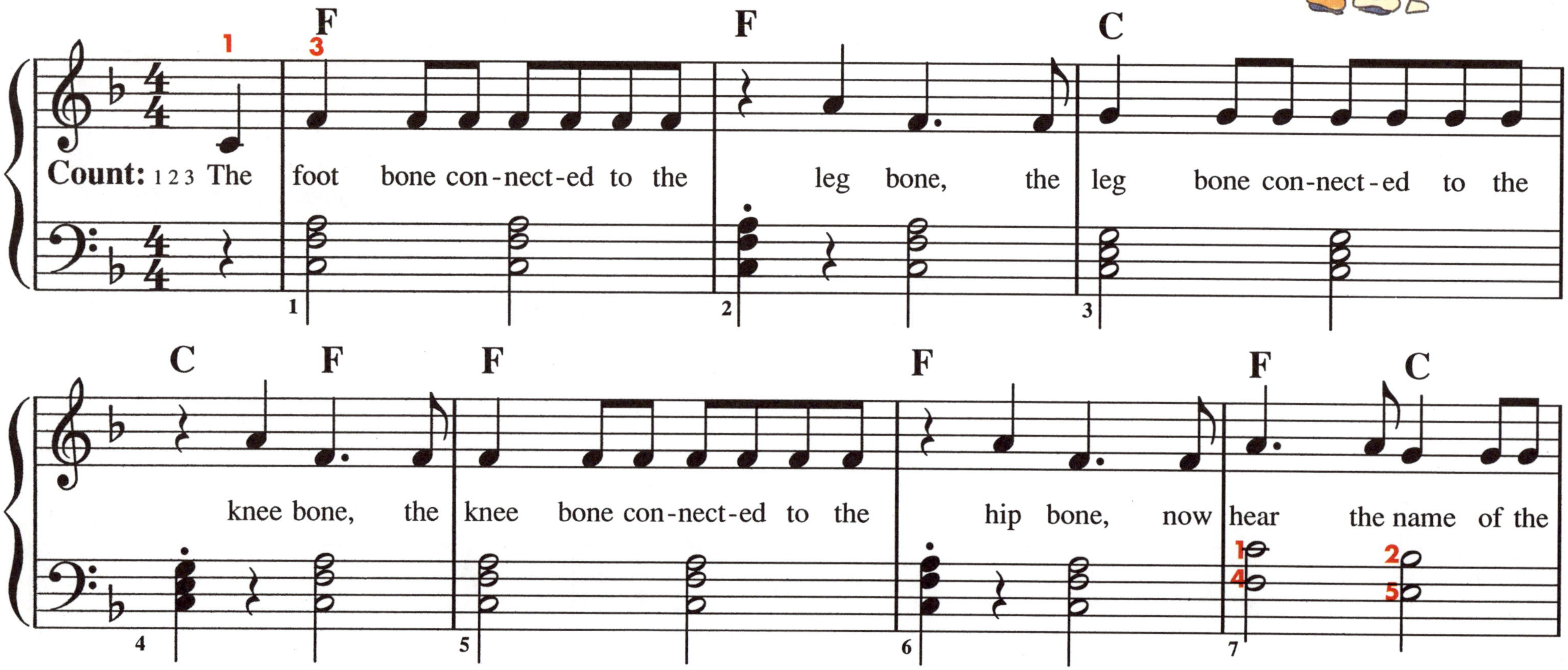

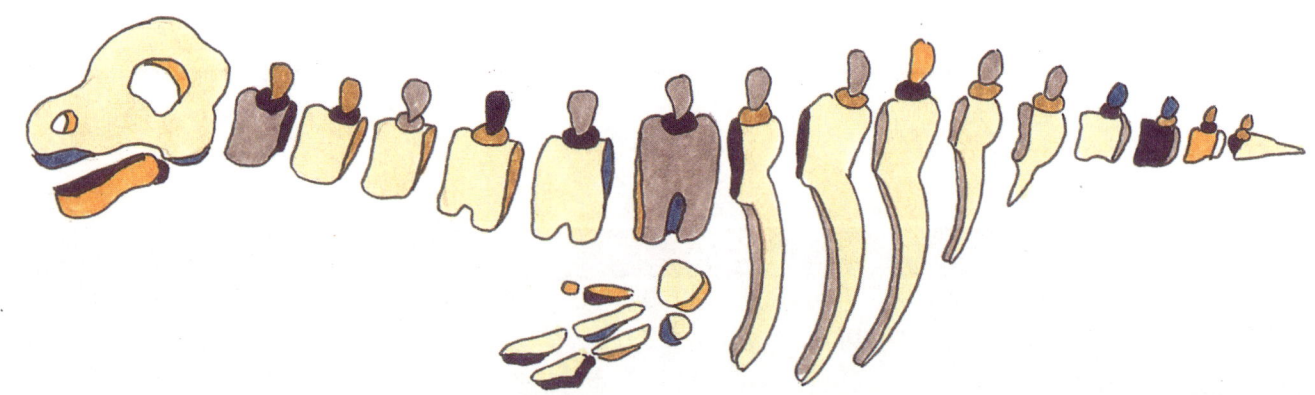

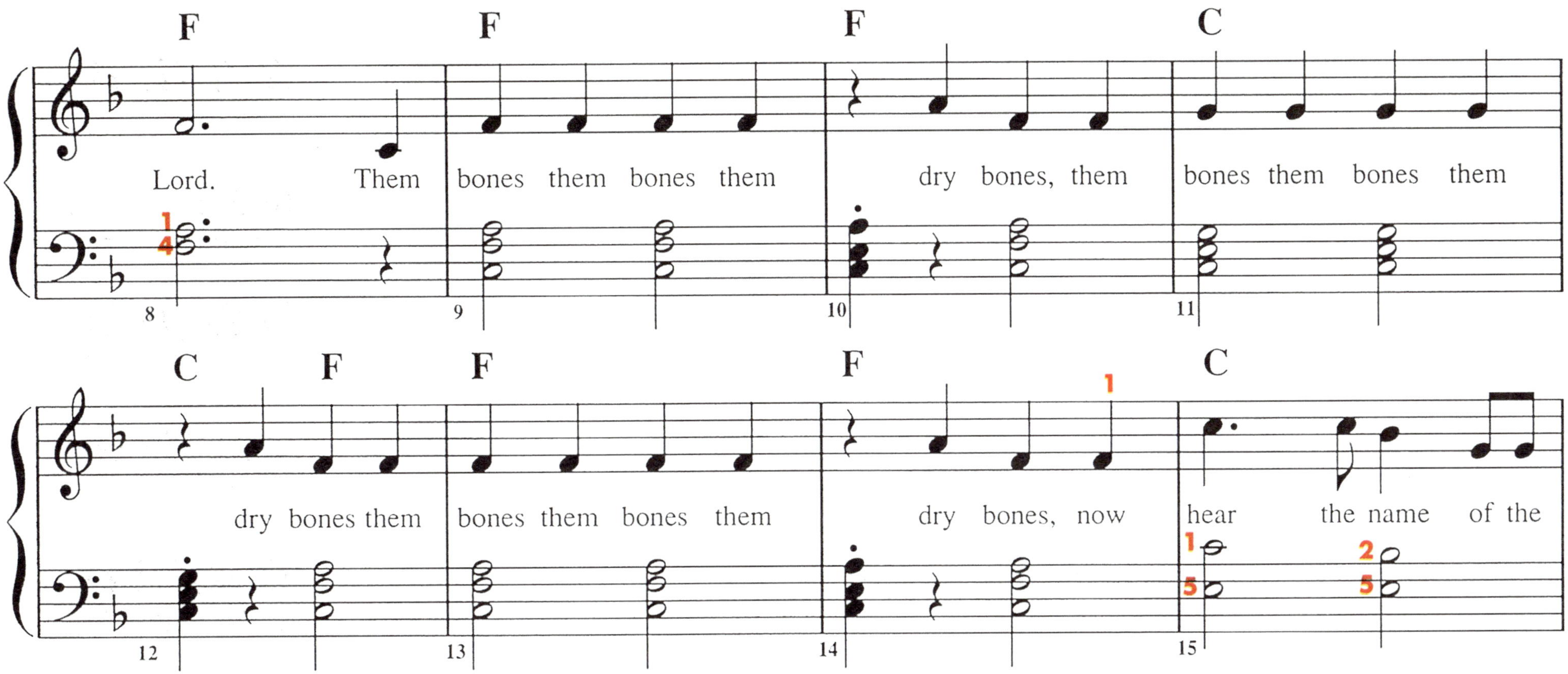

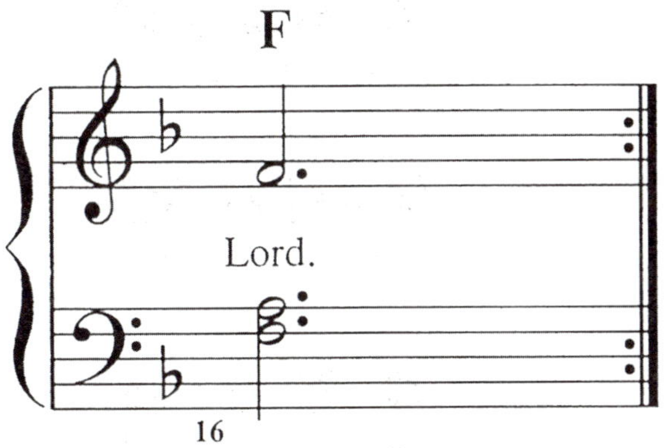

You can now play the songs on pages 46 to 48 of Supplementary Songbook C.

Notes and Rests

Note	Eighth Note (quaver)	Quarter Note (crotchet)	Dotted Quarter Note (dotted crotchet)	Half Note (minim)	Dotted Half Note (dotted minim)	Whole Note (semibreve)
Note	♪	♩	♩.	♩ (half)	♩. (dotted half)	o
Rest	𝄾	𝄽	𝄽.	▬	▬ 𝄽	▬
Number of Counts	$\frac{1}{2}$	1	$1\frac{1}{2}$	2	3	4

Chords

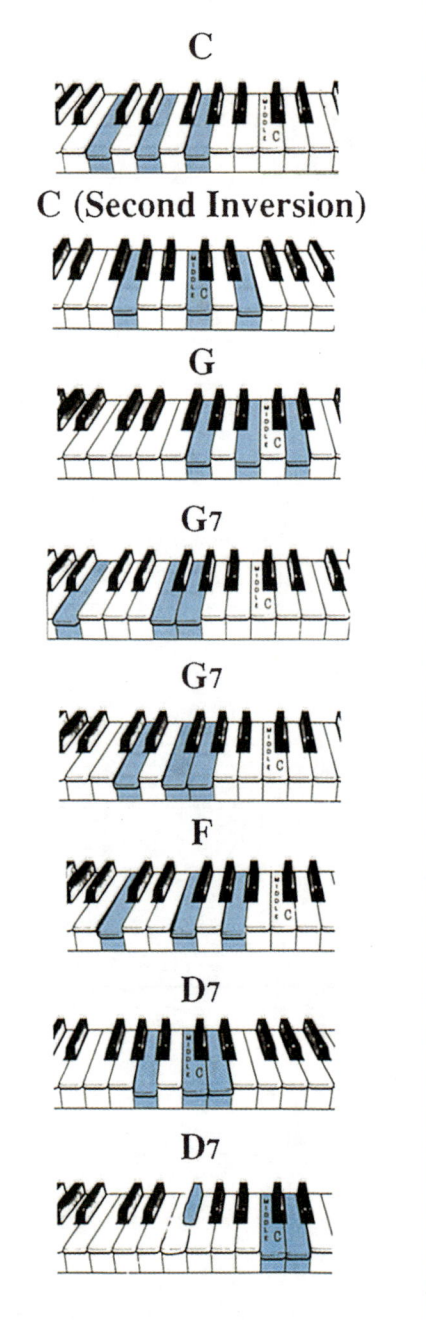

Notes on the Staff

Notes on the Keyboard

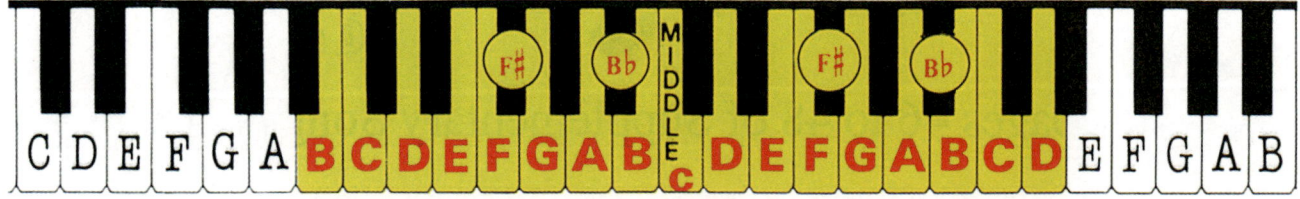